◀▌ The Black Crayon ▐▶

It's All About You
COLORING AND ACTIVITY BOOK

Written and Illustrated
by Erinn Sneed

When I Grow Up
PUBLISHING

When I Grow Up Publishing, Inc.

Copyright © 2017 by Erinn Sneed
Written, illustrated and cover designed by Erinn Sneed
Edited by Anita Rose Banks, Shirahba Rasheed and Rhonda Crowder

Cleveland, Ohio

ISBN-13   978-0-9795117-1-4
ISBN-10   0-9795117-1-2

In memory of:
Donald Sneed, Patricia Howard, Ronald Howard, Jewelene Gates, Ruth Bailey, Bernice Davis, Felix 'Jojo' Terrence, Raoof Muhammond, James Johnson Bey, Drew Bey, John Bey, Julius Bey, Elrod Bey, Dumis Bey, Will Peoples, George Jolly, Delores Dunn, Junior Davis, Darrell Thomas Bey, Michael Frost, Kai Wingo, Annie Grissom, Bill Potts, Matthew Whetstone

Special thanks to:
Betty Sneed, Lavonda Talbert, Anita Rose Banks, Steven E. Boyd, Danny Queen, Wayne Chandler (author of *Ancient Future*), Harvey Zay, Steven Howard, Ishmail Douglas, Sharlyn Howard, Elizabeth Taylor, Andre Taylor (author of *You Can Still Win*), Michelle 'Fenyx' Jackson, Bob Lanier, Jeff Phelps, John Phelps, Ronnie Duncan, Elisha Patterson, David Price, Jennifer Haliburton, RaShimba Bloom, Kevin 'Chill' Heard, Daria Hammond, Shirahba Rasheed

Special thanks to booksellers:
Jamie & Robin 'Lucy' Uptons, Bruce Bridges of the (KnowBookstore), Ms. Lisa & Mr. Turner of Africa Nations Imports, Mittie Jordan of Deuteromony Cafe 8:3, Sunny Sana, Roxanne Warner and Luther Warner of Lushena Books, AB World Books

Learn your history, your culture and who you are. Your ancestors brought knowledge to the world. Knowledge is power. Be strong.

" The world you want to live in and that you need to live in needs you to create it—it needs your input. The world needs to hear what you have to say. The last word has not been spoken…The last word has not been spoken." — **Beah Richards**

Beah Richards: 1920-2000
Actress, dancer and poet

"Everything you need, you've got ... it's there, perfect, complete—maybe not yet realized, but perfect and complete." — **Beah Richards**

When I grow up I can become an astronaut and travel in space. I could walk on the moon!

Read! Books hold the keys to the past and can unlock your future.

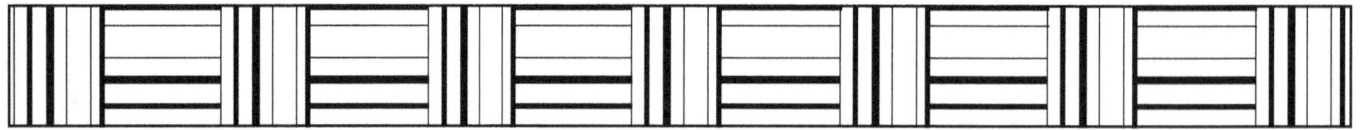

Back row (left to right): Uncle Rayheem, my mom; and our next door neighbor, Cliff.
Front row: My little sister, Isis; me (Tameka), and my friend, Shannon

Kwanzaa is the best time of year! It is a holiday that celebrates our African roots, culture and community with fun activities and gift-giving. It starts on December 26 and goes until January 1st.

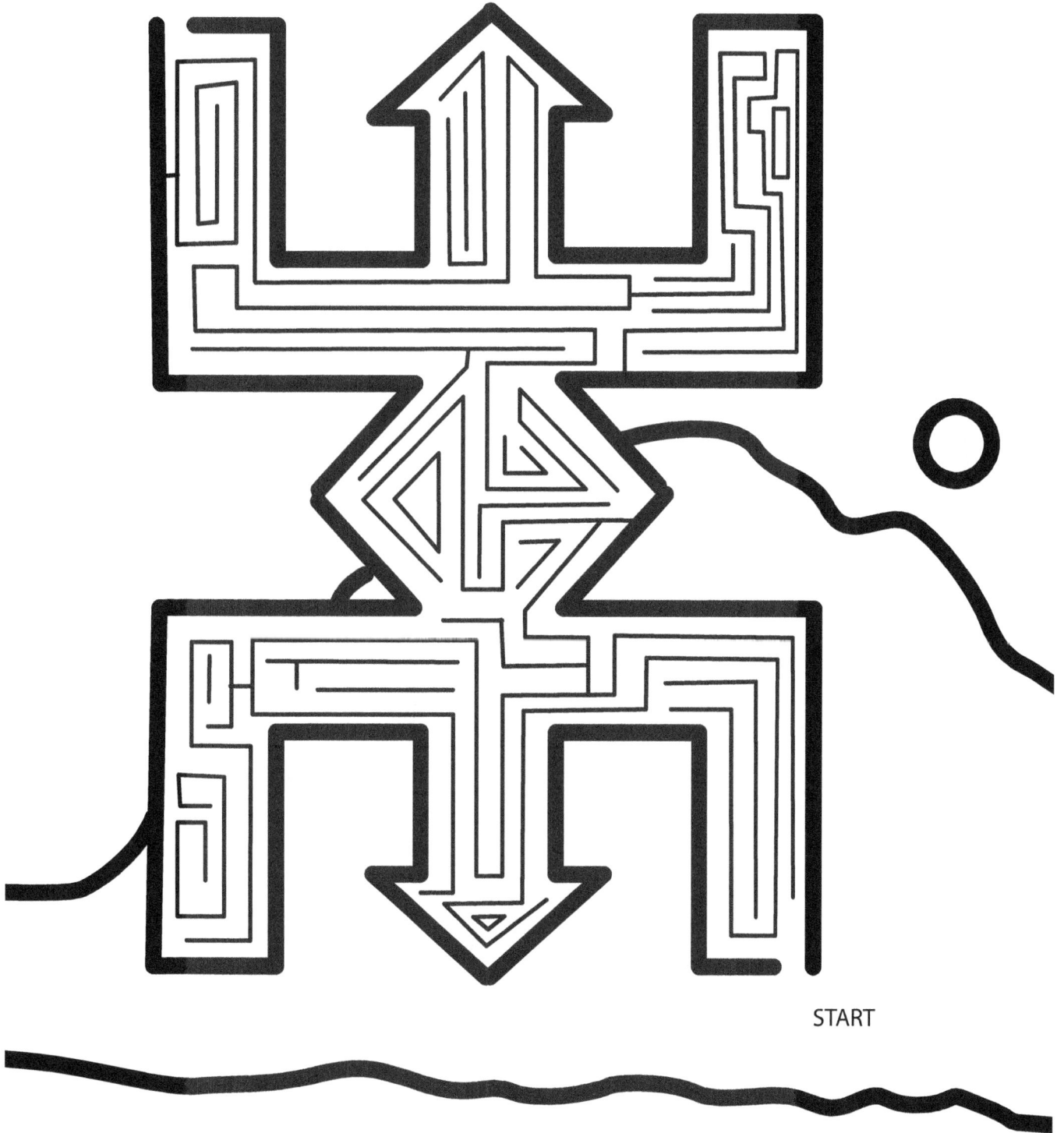

Maze

FINISH

START

This symbol means "Understanding."

Answer on page 40

We are Moors

Moors brought civilization to Spain, and were said to have brought Europe out of the Dark Ages.

What did you learn about yourself today?

It is good to learn about math, science, reading and other subjects. YOU are an important subject, too! Learn and KNOW Thyself!

INVENTIONS BY BLACK INVENTORS
Word Search Puzzle

```
E L E C T R I C L A M P B U L B O E S A E
U W T A B L A N T E R N A I N R E T T A L
W C R H I R Q B O Y V D R A L L O C E H E
E L A C C T R I R U S O A I M R F B T R V
E O F T Y E A R T O I N T I G K O E H D A
T T F L C R L R A L T Q A S S H L U O N T
F H I O L E T L O K I O A A G R D E S B O
I E C R E F R I U T I N M P G V I A C R R
H S L T F R I R P L R S A O C R N P O W Y
S D I N R I C O O E A N A D J E G T P Q U
R R G O A G Y N R G E R A T G R B E E N R
A Y H C M E C I E L I S P P G C E Y I E O
E E T T E R L N T S U N P H G D D B N P P
G R U A H A E G I H I M A I O R O O S N R
C I R T N T A B R L T N A I G N I R G I M
I P U S H O O O W E A T P U G T E E R A E
T U I O H R R A E L I N I I I W O E E T N
A Q U M G G A R P P I T A D O R S P H N O
M E J R B A O D Y L A N N M G A O M N U R
O O P E H T A R T R I O N I G T V I S O T
T T A H S H P V E L C W A I G S O R F F C
U E C T T F I S C R A S L S I M E A G R S
A O L R A B S R I L K N Y G G U B Y B A B
P H O N E T R A N S M I T T E R A B M R C
```

1.	Air Conditioner (Frederick M. Jones)	9.	Folding Bed (L. C. Bailey)	17.	Refrigerator (J. Standard)
2.	Automatic Gear Shift (Richard Spikes)	10.	Fountain Pen (W.B. Purvis)	18.	Stethoscope (Imhotep)
3.	Baby Buggy (W. H. Richardson)	11.	Gas Mask (Garrett Morgan)	19.	Stove (T.A. Carrington)
4.	Bicycle Frame (L.R. Johnson)	12.	Guitar (Robert F. Flemming, Jr.)	20.	Phone Transmitter (Granville Woods)
5.	Cellular Phone (Henry T. Sampson)	13.	Ironing Board (Sarah Boone)	21.	Thermostat Control (Frederick M. Jones)
6.	Clothes Dryer (G. T. Sampson)	14.	Lantern (Michael C. Harvey)	23.	Traffic Light (Garrett Morgan)
7.	Electric Lamp Bulb (Lewis Latimer)	15.	Lawn Mower (L.A. Burr)	24.	Tricycle (M.A. Cherry)
8.	Elevator—improvements (Alexander Miles)	16.	Motor (Frederick M. Jones)	25.	Typewriter (Burridge & Marshmann)

Answers on page 40

Adinkra Symbols

The Adinkra people of West Africa use ancient symbols to communicate ideas. There are nine Adinkra symbols in this picture. Can you find them all?

ADINKRAHENE
"Chief of Adinkra symbols" greatness, charity and leadership

NEA ONNIM
"Learning" You can become knowledgeable from study

AKOKONAN
"The leg of a hen" mercy, nurturing

MATE MASIE
"What I hear I keep" knowledge and wisdom.

OSRAM NE NSOROMMA
"The moon and the star" love and faithfulness

SANKOFA
"Return and get it" the value of learning from the past

DENKYEM
"Crocodile" adaptability.

MMUSUYIDEE
"Removes ill luck" good fortune and sanctity

SESA WORUBAN
"Change" I can change and transform my life

Answers on page 40

Women were the first farmers, doctors and recorders of time. They used a moon-based calendar (called a lunar calendar) that had 13 months. When they followed the moon's phases, women knew when to plant certain seeds, what herbs to give to treat illnesses and when a pregnant woman was due to give birth.

Funga Means "Welcome"

Funga is a traditional welcome dance performed by the Vai people of Liberia, a country on the western coast of Africa.

Kentucky Derby

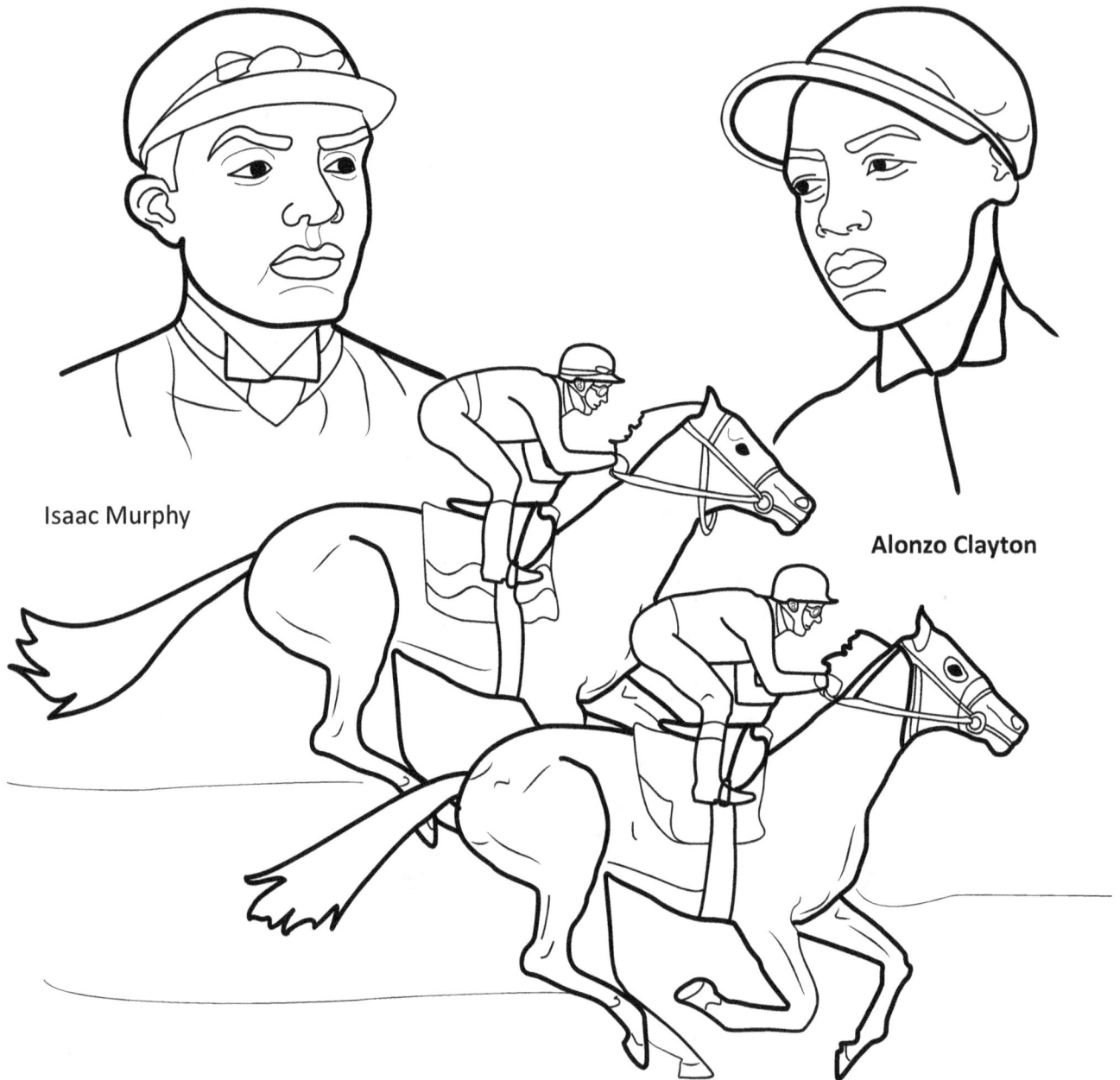

Isaac Murphy

Alonzo Clayton

15 of the first 28 Kentucky Derbys were won by black jockeys and 5 were trained by black trainers. www.about.com.

Oliver Lewis was the rider of the first Kentucky Derby winner Aristides.
Alonzo Clayton & James Perkins both won the Kentucky Derby at 15.
Jimmy Winkfield won the Kentucky Derby in 1901 and 1902.
Isaac Murphy is considered one of the greatest riders in American history, for being the first jockey to win three Kentucky Derbys.

The key to world peace is to have peace within yourself
Hotep (Egyptian) - As-salaam Alaikum (Arabic) - Alaafia (Yoruba) - Amani (Swahili)
Shanti (India) - Paz (Spanish) - Heping (Mandarin) - Shalom (Hebrew)
All of these words mean "Peace," so let peace be with you.

My little sister and I argue and fight sometimes, but we love each other very much.

"Every person is born into the world to do something unique and something distinctive, and if he or she does not do it, it will never be done." —**Dr. Benjamin E. Mays, U.S. Educator and Clergyman**

John W. Greene, Jr., was among the many black pilots who were viewed as pioneers in aviation. They formed a club called "The Cloud Club," and offered flying classes using the four aircraft they owned. By 1950, the airport they started, Columbia Air Center, had grown to be one of the most active airports in Prince George's County, Maryland.

Nigerian-born inventor Dr. Phillip Emeagwali is a famous African-American inventor, often called "Father of the Internet." After studying the way bees build and work within a honeycomb, he was inspired to create a similar network for computers to help forecast the weather. He used 65,000 processors to invent the world's fastest computer. His weather prediction technology is still used today.

I CAN!

I can be a doctor or a scientist.

My people built the Sphinx and the pyramids. I can build, too!

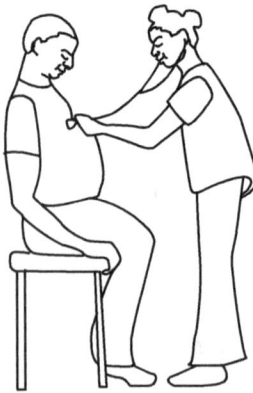

I can be an inventor, just like Alexander Miles, the man who created improvements to the elevator.

I can be a leader, just like Malcolm X and Martin Luther King, Jr.

I learn so much about my race during Black History Month! It makes me feel like I can do anything!

Black Wall Street

"Black Wall Street" (also known as "Little Africa") was a wealthy Black community in the 1920's located in Tulsa, Oklahoma. The people there owned 600 businesses, including restaurants, grocery stores, construction companies, hospitals, libraries, schools, a bank, a post office, a bus system and private airplanes.

Olmecs

This is a drawing of one of the six Olmec stone heads found in Mexico's forest. They are eleven feet tall and weigh up to twenty tons. The broad features suggest that the Olmecs may have been Africans. They traveled to Mexico about 1300 B.C. The Olmecs were mathematicians and astronomers, and also introduced writing to North America.

African American Oscar Winners

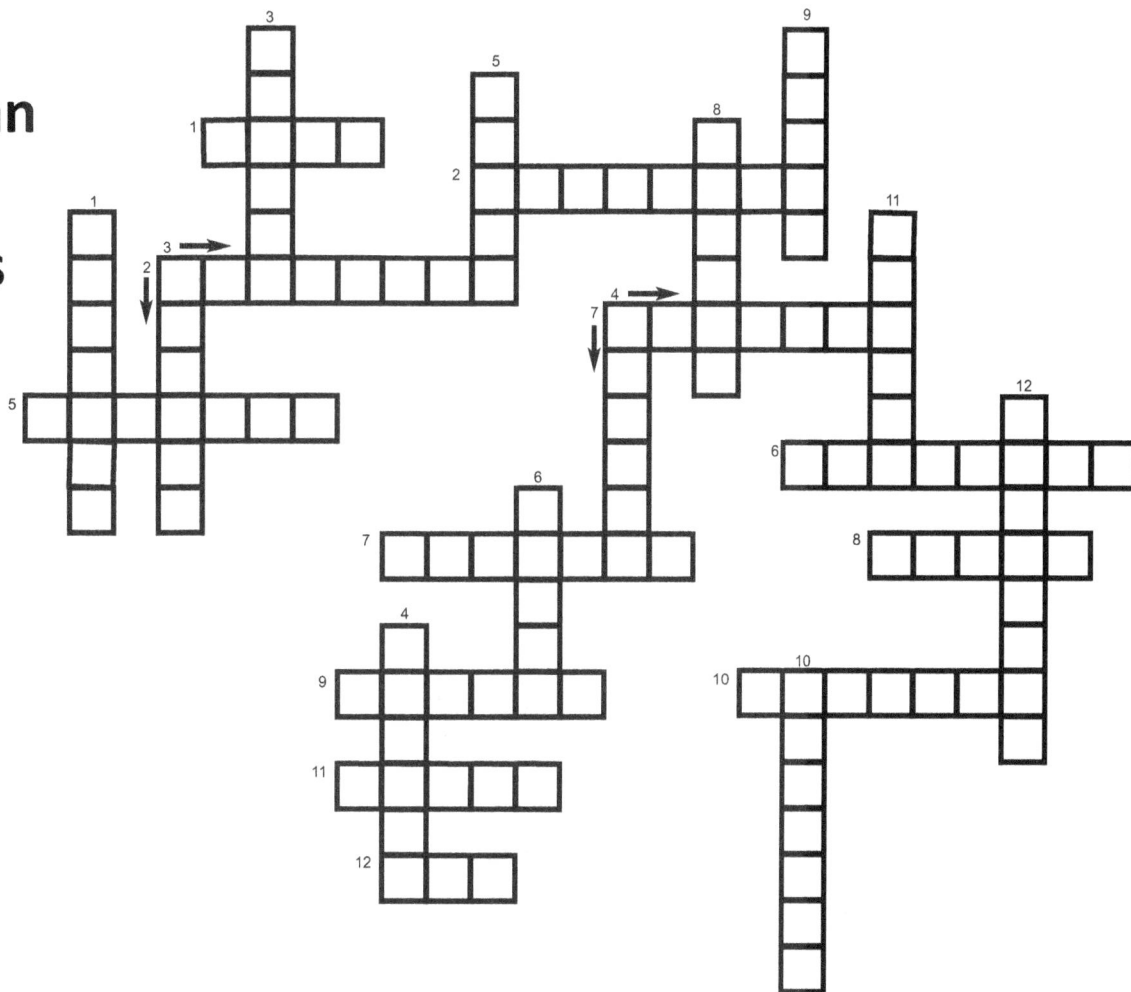

ACROSS

1. Jamie ___ won best actor for his portrayal of legendary singer Ray Charles in "Ray"(2004).

2. Hattie ___ was the first African American to win an Academy Award, for her role in "Gone With the Wind" (1939).

3. Russell ___ won two awards – for 1989's "Glory" and 1990's "Dances with Wolves" – in the category of Sound.

4. Morgan ___ was honored Best Supporting Actor for "Million Dollar Baby." (2005)

5. Cuba ___ Jr.'s performance as a veteran football player in "Jerry Maguire" (1996) earned him an Oscar.

6. Whoopi ___ , honored for her role in "Ghost" (1990) – is among a long list of comedians turned award-winning actors.

7. "An Officer and a Gentleman" (1982) made Louis ____ Jr. the first African-American man to win an Oscar for Best Supporting Actor.

8. Singer/actress ___ Cara not only sang "Flashdance ...What A Feeling" for the movie "Flashdance" (1984), she also won an Oscar for co-writing it.

9. Composer ___ Jones received the Jean Hersholt Humanitarian Award (1995).

10. Best Supporting Actress winner ___ displayed her acting skills in "Precious" (2010).

11. ___ Davis won Best Supporting Actress for her role in "Fences" (2017)

12. Mahershala ___ won Best Supporting Actor for his role in "Moonlight" (2017)

DOWN

1. Gifted musician/composer Herbie ___ was awarded for his soundtrack for "Round Midnight" (1986).

2. Stevie ___ 's song, "I Just Called to Say I Love You" (1984), earned him an Oscar.

3. ___ Richie's award-winning music on "White Nights" (1985) topped the charts.

4. ___ Nyong'o won Best Supporting Actress in "12 Years a Slave" (2017)

5. The role of Uncle Remus in "Song of the South" (1946) earned ___ Baskett an honorary award.

6. The soulful "Theme from Shaft" (1971) – earned ___ Hayes a Best Original Song award.

7. Best Actor ___ Whitaker played a dictator in "The Last King of Scotland" (2006).

8. ___ Poitier's performance in "Lilies of the Field" (1963) made him the first African American awarded as Best Actor.

9. ___ Berry won critical praise for her award-winning performance in "Monster's Ball" (2001).

10. ___ Spencer won Best Supporting Actress for " The Help" (2013)

11. Dramatic portrayals earned ___ Washington Oscars for "Glory" (1989) and "Training Day" (2001).

12. ___ Hudson won Best Supporting Actress for "Dream Girls" (2006)

Answers on page 40

My neighborhood is the best place to live!

When I grow up, I will go to college so that I can become a professional. Then, I will move back here to raise a family and help the people in our community.

Maze

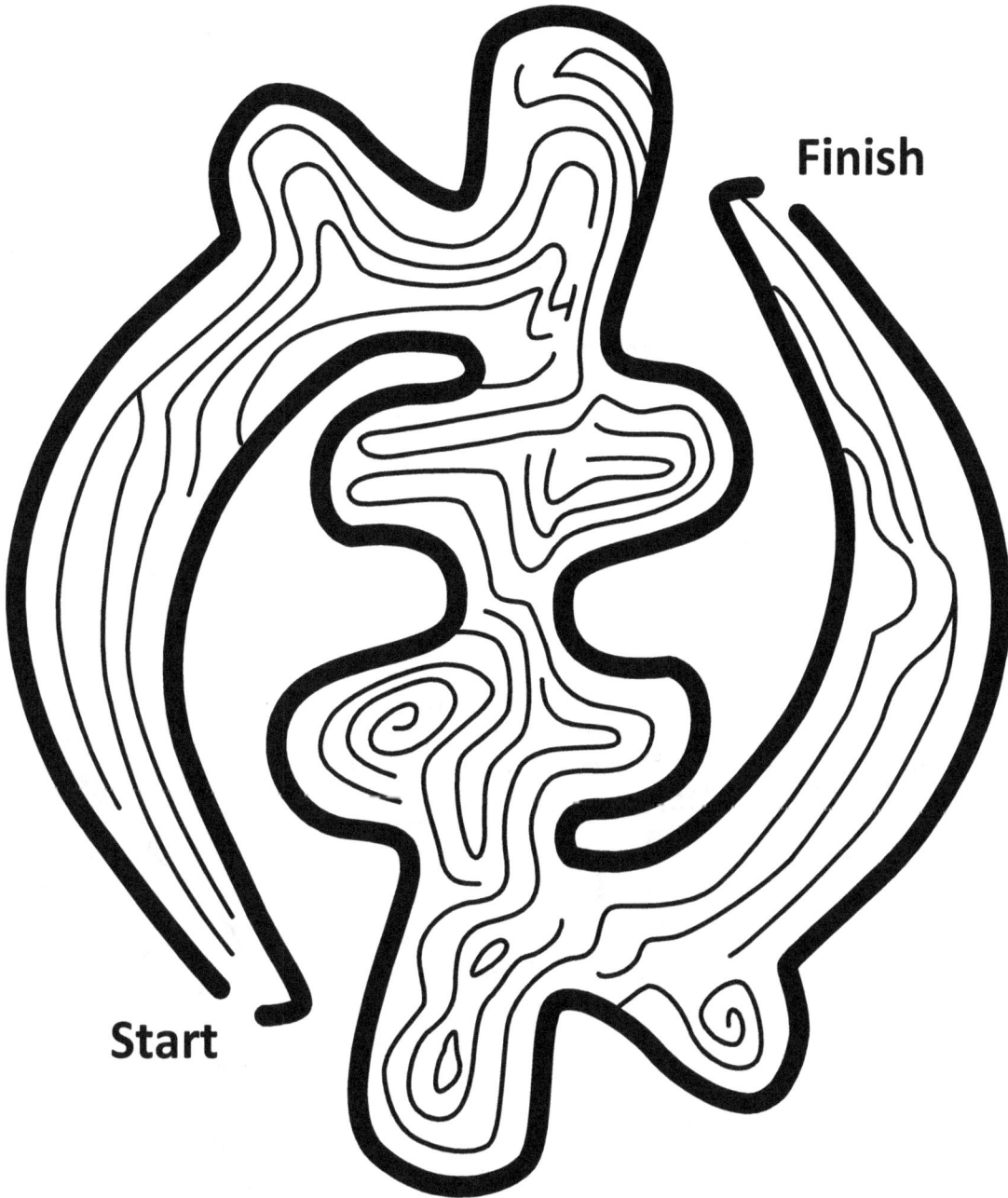

Finish

Start

GYE NYAME

An Adinkra symbol from Ghana meaning the supremacy of the Creator.

Answer on page 40

Dr. Mark Dean born 1957

You may have never heard of Dr. Mark Dean, but you probably see his work every day at your home or school. He was a very important player in creating the first Personal Computer (PC). The math whiz from Tennessee holds three of the original nine patents for the PC – as well as more than 20 additional patents!

Being smart and having an education — it's a black thing.

Black people were the first scientists, mathematicians, engineers and doctors on this planet.

Pouring LIBATION is a way of giving thanks to our ancestors.

Ashe: means "So Be It" in Swahili

Detective

To develop your detective skills, circle the picture on the right that is the same as the one on the left.

Answers on page 40

JUNETEENTH

On June 19, 1865, soldiers rode on horseback to Galveston, Texas to inform slaves that the Civil War was over and that they were free. However, this was almost three years after President Lincoln signed the decree that freed slaves across the United States. Today, we commemorate this with the holiday Juneteenth.

FAMILY REUNION

Future stars will be using micro technology developed by James West

Future Star

James West, born February 10, 1931, invented foil electret transducers, used in 90% of today's microphones.

Soul Food Word Search

Find in the puzzle the words that appear in bold in the word list. Look up, down, sideways, forward, backward, and diagonally for the foods you love to eat. Once you find the word, circle it in the puzzle and cross it off the list.

```
B C H I C K E N C O L L A R D G R E E N S
S L W A T E R M E L O N A I G R C S G R C
W T A K H K Q W P F S V R A S L O C M R P
E P R C M E C K A L E C A B B A G E G A I
E K E E K Q A T O L I U A T Y R N E G B Y
T H D T T E A R A G S N B R O H O A G N A
P O B E R C Y S O L I E A I M R S E G H Y
O K E P M T E E O K I N L G W E T A T R T
T V A L H E Y U D C R N A O B R H S U Y Y
A O N T S H U R O P I N A I C R N D R Q E
T S S A G R O R D I E N A B G E D E N R S
O T R T H C P B O L P A O I E A P L I R E
E I I V V O E F D S I C S R L R E U P S E
P R C T W A A A D N E N G A P R A E G N H
I G E X N C E O R H I D S I G R C J R A C
E M U S H R O Y T L R O A R U R H E E E I
S O U E B F O N R A T M P R M D C N E B N
R G U N A F O R T A P N A U B R O P N A O
S D R E Y N M S T O L F F Q O A B M S M R
S O S P R C U O R L D N A A F S B I S I A
C W U O H M P R E P J Q R I B D L R G L C
B E C A T F I S H L I K A I V U E H P R A
L O C R A B S R O K O N A X G M R S J M M
L E A F Y G R E E N V E G E T A B L E S C
```

1. Black Eyed Peas
2. Cabbage
3. Catfish
4. Chicken
5. Cornbread
6. Corn on the Cob
7. Cole Slaw
8. Collard Greens
9. Crabs
10. Grits
11. Gumbo
12. Kale
13. Leafy Green Vegetables
14. Lima Beans
15. Macaroni & Cheese
16. Mustard Greens
17. Okra
18. Peach Cobbler
19. Potato Salad
20. Red Beans & Rice
21. Seafood
22. Shrimp
23. Sweet Potato Pie
24. Squash
25. Turnip Greens
26. Watermelon
27. Yams

Answers on page 40

Kwame Ture, 1941-1998
Activist and Writer

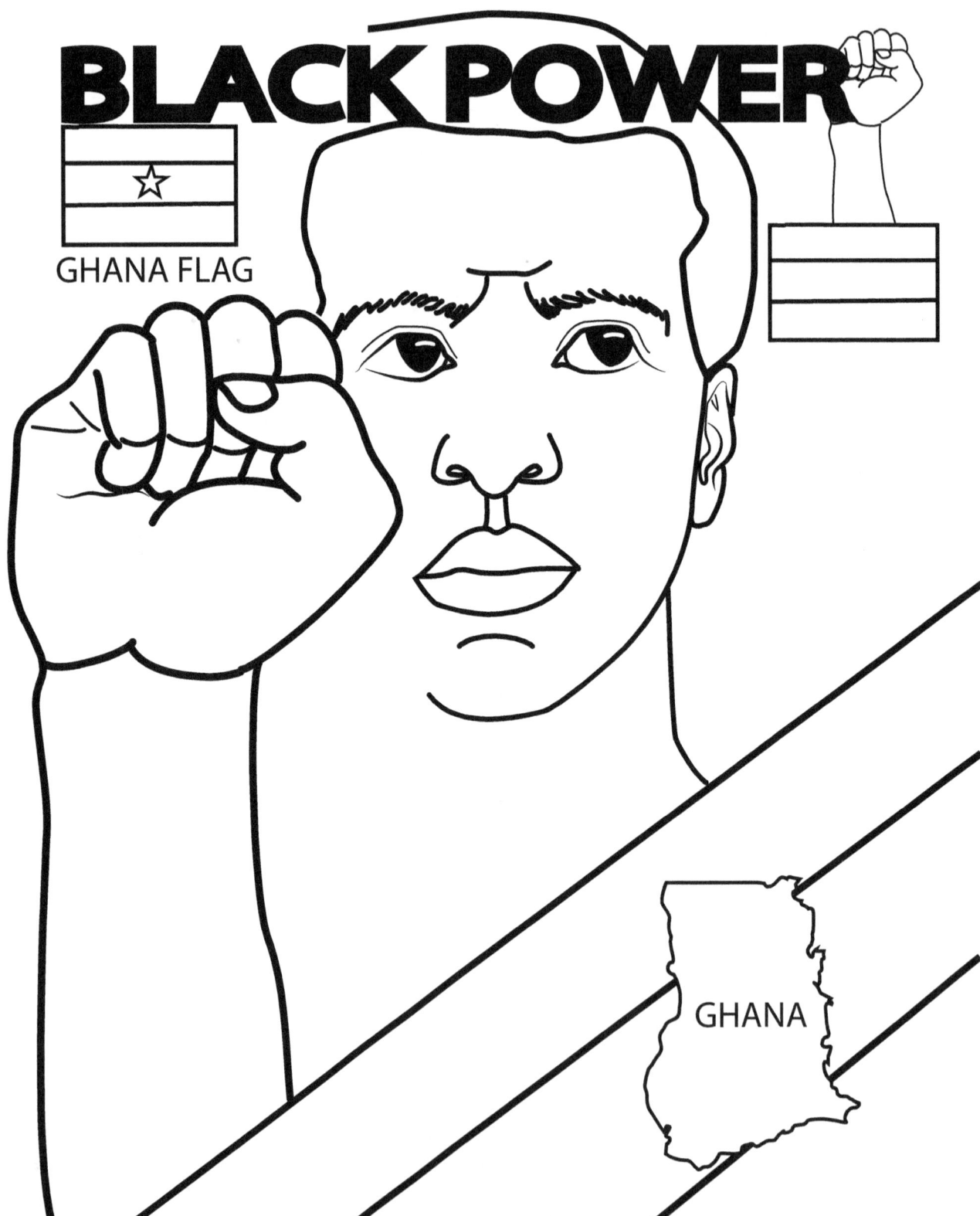

BLACK POWER

GHANA FLAG

GHANA

Kwame Ture (born Stokely Carmichael) made the phrase "Black Power" famous. He began fighting for equal rights while a student at Howard University in Washington, D.C. He was a member of the Black Panther Party: a group that promoted African American pride and independence during the 1960s and '70s. Later, he went to work for the All African People's Revolutionary Party in Ghana.

Ma'at and Me

Ma'at was the goddess of truth, balance, justice and order in ancient Egypt.

Answer Key

Understanding (from page 11)

Inventions by Black Inventors Word Search Puzzle (from page 14)

Adinkra Symbols (from page 15)

African American Oscar Winners (from page 27)

Gye Nyame (from page 29)

Finish

Start

Detective (from page 33)

Soul Food Word Search Puzzle (from page 37)

Fun Notes

Fun Notes

_____

_____

_____

_____

_____

_____

_____

_____

_____

_____

_____

_____

_____

_____

_____

_____

_____